Discover Great National Parks

YOSEMITE

Christine Petersen

Kids' Guide to History, Wildlife, Great Sequoias, and Preservation

© 2024 by Curious Fox Books™, an imprint of Fox Chapel Publishing Company, Inc., 903 Square Street, Mount Joy, PA 17552.

Discover Great National Parks: Yosemite is a revision of *Yosemite*, published in 2017 by Purple Toad Publishing, Inc. Reproduction of its contents is strictly prohibited without written permission from the rights holder.

Paperback ISBN 979-8-89094-072-8
Hardcover ISBN 979-8-89094-073-5

The Cataloging-in-Publication Data in on file with the Library of Congress.

To learn more about the other great books from Fox Chapel Publishing, or to find a retailer near you, call toll-free 800-457-9112 or visit us at www.FoxChapelPublishing.com.

We are always looking for talented authors. To submit an idea, please send a brief inquiry to acquisitions@foxchapelpublishing.com.

Fox Chapel Publishing makes every effort to use environmentally friendly paper for printing.

Printed in China

WELCOME

CHAPTER ONE
HIDDEN
TREASURE

Waterfalls tumble over high canyon walls. Rivers curve through green meadows and shady woodlands. Trees that stand as tall as giants and spectacular mountain peaks soar overhead. These are a few of the marvelous sights that bring millions of visitors to Yosemite National Park each year.

An Amazing Discovery

Yosemite is located in the Sierra Nevada mountain range in central California. Natural forces have shaped this mountain range over long stretches of time.

Native Americans first settled in Yosemite more than eight thousand years ago.[1] In the early nineteenth century, the Yosemite region was home to two tribes. Miwok Indians lived among the foothills on the western side of the Sierras. Paiute territory was near Mono Lake, in the desert east of the mountains.[2]

By 1822, the United States had only twenty-four states. All were located east of the Rocky Mountains. Most Americans had no idea what lay beyond. The rugged West

Rugged mountains, tree- and grass-covered valleys, and sparkling streams are commonplace in Yosemite.

5

Benjamin Bonneville

was controlled by Mexico. Few Americans had crossed it. U.S. Army captain Benjamin Bonneville was one of the first explorers to try. In 1832, he and a team followed rivers over the prairie and into the Rockies. There the party split up. Bonneville took some men with him to Oregon. A second group was led by his lieutenant, Joseph Walker. They went in search of a trail across California to the Pacific Ocean.

Late in the autumn of 1833, Walker's party reached the eastern foot of the Sierras. They followed Native American trails up the steep slopes. The men moved slowly through deep snow. They could only cover a few miles each day. High in the mountains, they came across an amazing sight: they saw streams running over the rocky landscape. The water seemed to fall off the edge of the earth. Peering down, the men saw a valley far below. Next, the explorers came to a grove of huge sequoia trees. Some measured more than 100 feet "round the trunk at the height of a man's head from the ground." Walker's men were the first white Americans to see the wonders of Yosemite Valley.[3]

Changing Too Quickly

Twenty-five years later, gold was discovered in the foothills west of Yosemite. Thousands of people came to California hoping to strike it rich. The Miwok and Paiutes fought to keep their homelands. Within a few years, most of California's remaining Native American tribes had been moved onto reservations or killed.

Yosemite Valley did not remain empty for long. In 1855, a group of tourists decided to visit this hidden wonderland. But it was not easy to get there! The trip required three days of travel on horseback or mule along rough trails. Waking on the first morning, visitor James Mason Hutchings saw the sun rise behind silvery rock walls, shining onto woodlands and green meadows filled with wildflowers. Sitting at the foot

James Mason Hutchings

of an impossibly tall waterfall, Hutchings had an idea. He would build a hotel there. He would "sell" Yosemite as a vacation spot.

One of his fellow tourists drew sketches of the valley. Hutchings wrote articles about the place. The story was printed in magazines nationwide.

Thomas Ayres's High Falls drawing was the first published image of Yosemite Valley. Hutchings called the waterfall Yo-Hamite Falls.

Although California had just become the 31st state in 1850, Americans in the east knew almost nothing about it. They were stunned to learn that such natural wonders had been found on the other side of the country.

Many other people saw ways to use Yosemite. Sheep ranchers allowed their herds to feed on sweet grasses and flowers in the high meadows. Miners dug up valuable minerals from the rocky mountain slopes. Farmers grew apples and other crops in the rich valley soil. Hotels, camps, and restaurants were built to feed and house tourists. The buzz of saws became a common sound, as loggers felled trees. The lumber was used to make buildings, fences, and furniture. The wood was used for fuel. Some giant sequoia trees were also cut down. A few were shipped to the East Coast and England. Crowds paid money just to stare at the gigantic logs.

A few people began to worry that Yosemite would be damaged by these changes. On March 28, 1864, a bill was introduced to Congress to protect Yosemite Valley and the Mariposa Grove of Giant Sequoias. No law of this kind had ever been written before. Congress and President Abraham Lincoln agreed to sign it, making the state of California responsible for protecting Yosemite. The land

A hole was cut through this tree so tourists could travel through it.

was set aside "for public use, resort and recreation" forever.[4]

Planning for the Future

In the summer of 1865, Frederick Law Olmsted and a group of men met in Yosemite Valley to discuss the future of California's new park. A few years earlier, Olmsted had built Central Park, a huge and beautiful public park in the middle of New York City. At this time, very few American cities had parks. Olmsted understood that city dwellers wanted a place to

Frederick Law Olmsted

exercise, relax, and be near nature. This was especially true for those who lived in crowded or dirty neighborhoods. He thought that everyone could enjoy such a park, and he was right. As soon as it opened, Central Park became the most popular place in New York City.

Olmsted believed that everyone should also be able to visit Yosemite. But how? Yosemite was high in the mountains. It was several days' ride by horseback from the nearest town. How could average Americans afford to visit this distant place? Olmsted suggested that better roads be built to replace the rough horse trails. One road should lead into the valley from towns west of Yosemite. Another could take visitors on a loop of sights around the valley floor. A separate road might connect the valley to the Mariposa Grove. He advised building cabins as free shelter for travelers along each route.

Olmsted knew that more people would visit Yosemite if there were more roads and services. "Before many years," he said, "these hundreds will become thousands and in a century the whole number of visitors will be counted by millions."[5] Yosemite must be protected as it became more popular, he said.

Other members of the park committee disagreed with this plan, so they hid his report. For many years, people continued to use Yosemite parklands however they wanted.

A New American Park

In 1868, a 30-year-old wanderer named John Muir arrived in San Francisco. He had read about Yosemite and wanted to see it. Muir was a talented inventor who had also studied science. He could fix or build almost anything. Most of all, Muir wanted to spend time in the wilderness. He climbed mountains and trees. He sat beside waterfalls to watch birds. He studied every detail of flowers. Muir even built a cabin over a tiny creek so he could always hear the bubbling of water and croak of frogs.

John Muir

Muir lived in Yosemite for six years (from 1868–1874), and he visited the park throughout his life. Like Olmsted, he worried that people were abusing Yosemite. Muir published magazine articles and books describing the park's natural beauty. He wanted other Americans to treasure this remarkable place, even if they never saw it in person. Muir made important friends who also supported his efforts. The Yellowstone region of Wyoming had been declared America's first national park in 1872. Could the same be done for Yosemite?

PEOPLE OF THE VALLEY

When gold miners asked the Miwok what the valley was called, they said *Yosemite*. The miners misunderstood the word. They thought it meant "grizzly bear." Later, language experts figured out that *Yosemite* meant "those who kill." The Miwok and Paiute had been enemies.

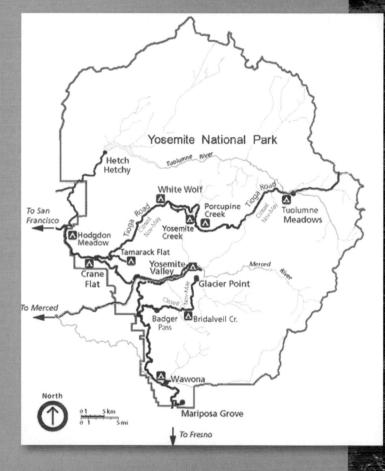

The valley tribe had a different name for their home—*Ahwahnee.* This meant "place of the gaping mouth."[6] The name describes the tunnel-like shape of Yosemite Valley. The valley is seven miles long. It is only one mile at its widest. The tribe called themselves the Ahwahneechee. This meant "People of the Valley."

Chapter Two
WELCOME TO
YOSEMITE

On October 1, 1890, Yosemite was officially named America's third national park. The government protected a block of land the same size as Rhode Island. It surrounded Yosemite and the Mariposa Grove of Giant Sequoias.

Ranchers, loggers, and miners did not want to give up their land. Army soldiers were sent to patrol the park. They were known as a "peacekeeping army." Among them were African-American troops. They were nicknamed Buffalo soldiers. They had served the United States during the Civil War. In many ways, these soldiers were the first park rangers. They protected Yosemite's wildlife, woodlands, and other natural resources. They even fought wildfires.

Many of the park's roads were built for stagecoaches during this era. In 1913, cars were allowed into Yosemite. Just as Olmsted had forecast, Yosemite was flooded with people. One million people visited in 1954. Today, the park hosts three to four times that many visitors each year.

Yosemite National Park celebrated its 125th anniversary in 2015. By then, it included 1,169 square miles of

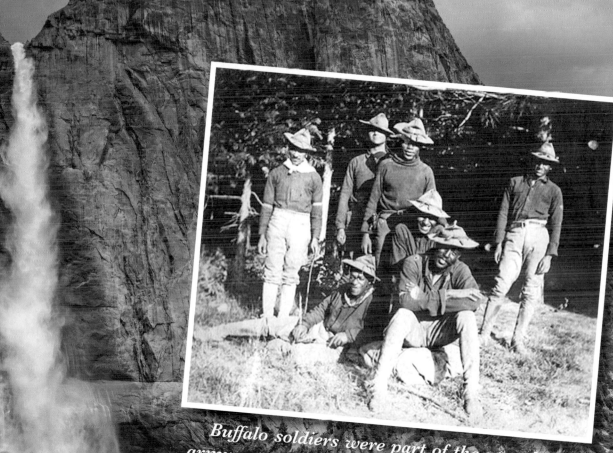

Buffalo soldiers were part of the peacekeeping army sent to Yosemite as the first park rangers.

mountains, forests, and meadows. There were more than 280 miles of paved and gravel roads within the park. People hiked along the 800 miles of trails that reached throughout the park.[2] Many of those paths had been made by army patrols more than a century before.

Today, hundreds of people hike into Yosemite National Park along the Pacific Crest Trail every year. This route runs north to south for 2,650 miles. It reaches from the Mexican border to Canada.[3] It passes through Yosemite's backcountry. This barely touched region is too steep and rugged for roads.

Yosemite's Regions

Yosemite's Arch Rock and Big Oak Flat are located on the park's western edge. Roads wind slowly up into the western foothills of the Sierra

Visitors can enter the park through the famous Arch Rock Entrance.

Nevada. They pass through historic gold-mining towns, such as Groveland and Mariposa.

Western Yosemite has the lowest elevation in the park. Very little snow falls there. The summer is long. Tall grasses cover the foothills like a living carpet. The grass may look brown, but it is not dead. Its roots reach deep down to find water. When springtime rains fall, the grasses burst into brilliant color again.

After a rainy spring, orange and purple wildflowers add splashes of color throughout the Yosemite valleys.

Wildflowers pop up across the hillsides. They look like splotches of paint on a canvas. Tangerine-colored California poppies, scarlet Indian paintbrush, and multi-hued lupines decorate the ground.

Red-barked manzanita shrubs form tangled thickets on steep hillsides. Manzanitas are evergreen. They keep their leaves year-round instead of losing them in autumn. The leaves are thick, with a waxy coating. They hold water even during the driest summer months.

In Spanish, *manzanita* means "little apple." It's a perfect description of the plant's small fruit. Deer, squirrels, and other animals find them delicious. So did Native Americans. They ate manzanita berries fresh, dried, and in a juice. They crushed manzanita leaves to cure stomachaches and to rub on poison oak rashes.

From Arch Rock and Big Oak Flat, the landscape rises into forested mountains.

Wawona is higher in the mountains. It gets more snowfall in winter. Summer temperatures are not quite as fierce. That slight difference in climate changes the habitat. Instead of grassland, a mixed forest of tall trees grows. The most common are deciduous oak trees and needle-bearing pine, fir, and cedars. They provide shade on warm summer days. They slow the wind during snowshoe hikes.

Massive California black oaks deal with winter by shedding their wide, flat leaves. If they did not, the leaves would hold snow. This weight would snap the stiff branches. Pine, fir, and cedar trees are evergreen. Their branches bend when piles of snow grow too heavy. Snow slips right off their flat, waxy needles and falls to the ground.

This cabin looks like a toy compared to these massive sequoia trees.

From Tioga Pass Entrance Station, visitors are treated to majestic views. They will also pass stone buildings that were built in the 1930s.

This is also the perfect altitude for giant sequoia trees to grow. The trees in the Mariposa Grove of Giant Sequoias stand as tall as skyscrapers. Some of them are up to 1,800 years old , and the Grizzly Giant is estimated to be about 3,000 years old.[4]

Tioga

Tioga Pass Entrance Station is located on the far eastern border of Yosemite National Park. Tioga Road runs east to west from the Tioga Pass toward Big Oak Flat. This is one of the most scenic roads in America. Soaring mountains and smooth-topped rock domes rise up all around.

CHAPTER ONE

The snow in Yosemite turns the park into a magical, wintry world.

Water gathers in low spots to form meadows, streams, and shallow lakes. The air is clear and fresh. The sky is brilliant blue.

The park's valley gets about an average of twenty-nine inches of snowfall during the winter season. Only a thin layer of snow covers the ground during most winter days. In the high country, an average of 288 inches of snow falls per year. In 1969, it reached a record depth of 323.9 inches! Between mid-November and late May, snowplows struggle to keep the high, winding road clear of snow.

In the foothills, it is too hot and dry for trees to grow. High in the mountains, trees also struggle due to long, cold, snowy winters. Slender lodgepole pine trees, white-barked aspens, and fluffy-looking hemlocks grow in patches instead of dense forests. Junipers manage to grow on bare rocks. Their twisted roots reach into cracks to find moisture and bits of soil.

THE BIG TREES

Sequoias begin life as papery seeds the size of flattened rice grains. To sprout and grow, the seed needs moist soil and patchy sunlight. During its first century of life, the young tree may grow two feet (0.6 m) per year.[5] It will continue to grow every year for the rest of its long life. In Yosemite's Mariposa Grove, the tree called the Grizzly Giant measures about 209 feet.[6] A single branch is as much as seven feet in diameter. Neighboring

The giant sequoias.

ponderosa pines and white fir trees can grow as high, but none of them have trunks as wide as the Grizzly Giant's branch.[7]

In 1903, John Muir brought President Theodore Roosevelt to see the Mariposa Grove. "These are the big trees, Mr. Roosevelt," said Muir proudly. The two men talked and listened to birdsong as they wandered through the grove. They looked up into the green cloud of leaves blocking the sky above. The president declared that Mariposa Grove was "the greatest forest site" of all. In 1906, he signed a law joining Yosemite Valley and Mariposa Grove with the surrounding national park.[8]

CHAPTER THREE
A CHANGING
LANDSCAPE

Yosemite is so amazing that it is easy to wonder what created such an unusual landscape. The short answer is rock, water, and time.

The Sierra Nevada range has not always been there. A series of volcanic eruptions began about 200 million years ago. Instead of flowing onto the surface, the hot magma cooled in pockets underground. When the eruptions died down about fifty million years ago, a line of rolling hills was left.[1] On the surface was a layer of soft rocks. Trees and other plants grew there. Animals made homes. Streams flowed over the surface. It was hard to imagine that huge, rocky domes of granite and other volcanic rock lay just below.

Over millions of years, water and wind caused the soft surface rocks to erode. As they wore away, the harder volcanic rock was slowly revealed. Movements inside Earth sped up this process. Earthquakes jolted the eastern side of the Sierra Nevada upward. As it did, the Merced River began to flow more rapidly to the west. Its

The Sierra Nevada range measures 430 miles in length, making it almost as big as the French, Swiss, and Italian Alps combined.

fast-moving waters dug deep into the landscape. It cut the beginnings of Yosemite Valley. The new valley cut off streams that once flowed north to south. They became waterfalls.[2]

When John Muir began exploring Yosemite in the 1860s, he saw clues that glaciers had changed the landscape. A glacier is a large body of ice formed as layers of snow pack together over time. Like a river of ice, glaciers flow slowly downhill under their own weight. Muir found many signs of ancient glaciers. There were long scratches in some high country rocks where glaciers had dragged pebbles along their surfaces. Other rocks were as shiny as mirrors. The glaciers had worn them smooth. He saw boulders scattered randomly, far from any mountain. These had also been carried along by glaciers. They had been left behind when the ice melted.[3]

John Muir did much to preserve the land at Yosemite.

Lyell Glacier was discovered by John Muir and was believed to be the largest glacier in the park. What remains of it today is generally considered to be an ice field.

Not everyone believed Muir's theory. That changed when Muir found glaciers in the mountains of Yosemite. These glaciers have been melting over the past 10,000 years. Some experts fear they may disappear before the end of the twenty-first century.[4]

Modern scientists have figured out that the first glacier flowed through Yosemite about two to three million years ago. Deep and incredibly heavy, it scraped into the valley floor and dug at its walls. The climate warmed. The ice melted. New glaciers formed and melted again. This cycle continued until about 20,000 years ago. Meltwater from the last glacier left a lake. Over time, it dried up. The flat meadows and woodlands of Yosemite Valley grow on soil that once lay on the bottom of that lake.[5]

Hetch Hetchy Reservoir is found in the northwestern part of Yosemite.

Yosemite has a second deep, glacier-carved valley. Hetch Hetchy Valley is located north of the Big Oak Flat entrance gate. In 1913, President Woodrow Wilson signed a bill allowing construction of a large dam across the valley's river.[6] Some people did not approve of this new dam. Known as preservationists, these people felt that humans should not interfere with nature. Although the dam was still built, the public gave more thought to how important it is to protect nature. When the dam was finished, Hetch Hetchy Valley filled with water. Today it is a reservoir, providing water to the city of San Francisco.

OUT OF CONTROL

Natural habitats can survive and even thrive after enduring natural wildfires. Human-caused fires are different. They often start closer to settled areas. They put nature, property, and lives at risk. Firefighters work to locate and put out these blazes as quickly as possible. Once in a while, a fire gets out of control and it may burn for days or weeks. The habitat may be seriously damaged and take years to recover.

The Stanislaus National Forest is a huge wilderness area located just west of Yosemite. Like the national park, it contains beautiful grasslands, forests, and mountains. This region suffers from drought. Fire crews must be on high alert. They watch daily for signs of fire.

In mid-August 2013, a fire was spotted in the Stanislaus. A hunter's campfire had spread, thanks to hot weather and wind.[7] Soon the blaze reached Yosemite. Thousands of firefighters rushed to help. Many came from other states. They fought the fire for nine weeks. When it was finally put out, 402 square miles of wilderness and parkland had burned. More than one hundred buildings were destroyed.[8]

The fire spread rapidly in the tree tops.

Chapter Four
HOME SWEET PARK

Hundreds of plant and animal species live in Yosemite National Park. It is a true wildlife wonderland, providing a variety of habitats.

Grassland

In Yosemite's western grasslands, animals are used to hot, dry weather. Grass- and seed-eating animals live there. Mice and chipmunks skitter along the ground. At sunrise or sunset, jackrabbits and mule deer often stand in the fields. Bobcats are one of the top predators in the grassland. They hunt small mammals, birds, and insects.

Covered in spiny scales, the western fence lizard looks fierce despite its small size. But it is harmless. It is also colorful! A gray-and-brown patchwork pattern marks its back. The belly and throat are blue. The fence lizard darts from rock to rock in search of small insects to eat. It often stops to rest and warm its body in the sun. When a predator approaches a male fence lizard, it does pushups to show off its blue belly. It hopes to scare the predator away with this flash of color.

Bobcats and western fence lizards make their home in Yosemite.

Woodland

One of Yosemite's most common birds is the acorn woodpecker. This robin-sized bird lives among oak trees. It has black-and-white feathers and a bright red head. Acorn woodpeckers use their long, strong bills to pound round holes in dead trees and power poles. They collect acorns and then stuff one acorn into each hole. This way, they are prepared for winter. Their squawking laughter echoes across the landscape.

Coyotes roam through many parts of Yosemite, but they like the woodlands best. These medium-sized mammals usually hunt small mammals like mice, voles, and squirrels. Sometimes they also scavenge, eating the meat of animals that have already died. Coyotes mate and stay together for life. The pair and their pups keep in touch by high-pitched howls and yips.

The acorn woodpecker eats insects, as well as acorns and other seeds.

Coyotes are also known as "song dogs" because of their many calls.

The American dipper hunts underwater, no matter the weather. Downy feathers keep it warm, and scales that cover the nostrils help the bird stay underwater for a long time.

Meadow

One of John Muir's favorite animals was the American dipper. This small bird lives next to fast-running streams and rivers. It nests on mossy rocks beside the water or behind waterfalls. Dippers stand on rocks, bobbing their heads to look underwater. If they see food, the birds dive under. They can swim against the current to catch it.

The mountain beaver spends its life in the water. Standing no more than fourteen inches tall, this mammal builds long tunnels leading to underground nests. It lives in groups of up to thirty beavers.[1] Mountain beavers are nocturnal, coming out at night in search of food. Daylight

Bighorn sheep are a common sight in the higher elevations of the park.

reveals where they have chewed down shrubs and small trees near their dens.

Mountain

Few species can live high in the mountains. It is too cold, and the rocky landscape prevents many plants from growing. The Sierra Nevada bighorn sheep is no typical animal. Its hoofed feet have pads on the bottom. This allows the animal to cross steep slopes without slipping. Even the tiniest lambs are excellent climbers. Bighorn sheep wander where no other animal can, searching for grassy food. They are an endangered species.

Change

During the ice ages, Yosemite and the surrounding area were home to some very different animals. There were short-faced bears that stood taller than a man, even when walking on four feet. Columbian mammoths looked like gigantic, furry elephants. Long-necked relatives of camels roamed the grasslands.[2] These creatures died out about 10,000–13,000 years ago, when the environment warmed up at the end

Scientists are unsure how furry Columbian mammoths were. The tusks of these ancient elephants could grow to sixteen feet long.

of the last ice age and humans invaded North America, hunting them and other large animals for food.

The great gray owl is one of California's rarest birds. About 200–300 live in California, with sixty-five percent of them in Yosemite National Park.

Some of the species in Yosemite today could suffer a similar fate. Over the past century, Earth's climate has grown rapidly warmer. People use fossil fuels every day to power factories and vehicles. These fuels include coal, oil, and natural gas. When burned, they release carbon dioxide and other gases. The gases rise into the atmosphere. They form a kind of shield that traps heat close to the planet's surface.

Many Yosemite species will be affected by climate change. For example, the pika (a relative of the rabbit) lives only on mountainsides where temperatures stay cool even in summer. Rainbow trout need chilly streams to survive. Pacific tree frogs lay their eggs in shallow ponds. These species may not survive in a warmer, drier climate.

Yosemite is also home to most of California's rare great gray owls. These birds nest in holes inside dead trees. In a warmer climate, wildfires will be more common. Dead trees may burn, leaving fewer nesting sites for the owls and other wildlife.

THERE'S A BEAR!

Many people go their whole lives without seeing a wild bear. In Yosemite, bear sightings are common. Hundreds of black bears live there.[3] Wherever a bear appears, traffic stops! People are excited to see these big animals. It's important to never go near a bear, even in a public area. A bear might feel threatened and attack.

Black bears hibernate in winter, but wander freely through the park the rest of the year. They eat berries, nuts, and grasses. Bears dig in the ground and under fallen logs to find insect larvae, a good source of protein. Bears also love honey! When they find a beehive, they often eat the whole thing—bees and all.

Bears in Yosemite Valley have lived near people for generations. That has led to some bad habits. Valley bears pull food from garbage cans. They even rip into tents and break car windows if they smell food. Campers have learned to use bear-proof storage containers provided in every campground. Others keep food in closed boxes inside the car.

Black bears have long claws that help them climb and hunt.

CHAPTER FIVE
EXPLORING
THE PARK

Yosemite is unlike any other place on earth. The valley's incredibly steep cliffs rise up like the crooked walls of a hallway built for a giant. Waterfalls are white ribbons against the gray-brown rock. Trees cover the valley floor and rocky slopes. A green river wanders between them. It flows the entire length of the valley.

Countless painters, photographers, and artists have tried to capture Yosemite on canvas or film. A famous oil painter named Albert Bierstadt journeyed to Yosemite. He took photographs and later made huge paintings from them. His art reflected more than the park's landscape. They glowed with the same feeling of wonder that Yosemite inspired in people who saw it.

Yosemite Valley is as beautiful as a painting. It is also a real place that people can explore. Visitor centers offer maps. They also have packets for children to earn a national park patch. Yosemite Village has museums and art galleries. A shuttle takes people on the loop road around the valley floor, which leads to many of the park's most famous natural features.

Albert Bierstadt's 1864 painting **Valley of the Yosemite** *is a famous image of the park.*

Yosemite Falls is one of the world's highest waterfalls. It plummets down 2,425 feet. El Capitan is the largest block of solid granite rock anywhere. It rises over 3,000 feet above the valley floor. People come from around the world to climb this difficult cliff. It takes several days to reach the top. Climbers must sleep in hammocks hanging high on the cliff face.

Bridalveil Falls is across the Merced River opposite El Capitan, alongside the sharp-topped Cathedral Rocks. Standing proudly at the

The southwest face of El Capitan. There are more than 250 routes to the top of this famous rock, but all of them are extremely difficult.

Half Dome's drop-off is four times higher than the Empire State Building.

east end of the valley is Half Dome. This massive rock looks like it has been sliced in half. The front side is almost vertical. The back and sides are rounded. A visit to Glacier Point gives tourists an incredible view of Yosemite Valley far below.

Great summer activities throughout the park include hiking, fishing, and rafting. Yosemite Valley offers a stable with rental horses and mules. Rangers lead guided walks and fireside talks at sites around the park. Swimmers enjoy diving into swimming holes along the Merced River in Yosemite Valley and near Wawona. Others take the Tioga Road to Tenaya Lake. The water is made from melted snow. It is clean—but cold! There is so much wildlife in Yosemite, visitors never know what animals they might spot on their trip.

Herds of elk roam the grasslands of Yosemite's valley areas.

The fun continues in winter. Yosemite Valley has an ice-skating rink. There is a beautiful forest perfect for snowshoeing and cross-country skiing. Skiers and snowboarders also enjoy Badger Pass, California's oldest ski area.

With its waterfalls, mountain peaks, giant trees, and huge meadows, it is no surprise that over three million people come to Yosemite each year.[1] No matter what they do there, they are sure to go home with memories to last a lifetime.

Yosemite Falls are the highest falls in the park, cascading some 2,425 feet. That is nearly half a mile!

FUN FACTS

- Yosemite is located in the Sierra Nevada of eastern California.
- People have lived in Yosemite Valley for as long as 8,000 years.
- Yosemite National Park was founded on October 1, 1890. It was America's third national park.
- In 1906, Yosemite Valley and Mariposa Grove of Giant Sequoias were added to Yosemite National Park.
- Every year, the park welcomes between three to five million visitors.
- Nine percent of visitors are from other nations, while ninety-one percent are from the United States. Of U.S. visitors, eighty-nine percent live in California.
- The park covers an area of 1,169 square miles.
- Nearly ninety-five percent of Yosemite National Park is designated as wilderness area.
- The park's lowest point is the Merced River at 2,105 feet. Yosemite's highest elevation is the summit of Mount Lyell at 13,014 feet.
- There are countless waterfalls in the park, but how many there are exactly depends on seasonal rainfall and snowfall, as well as when you visit!

FUN FACTS

- The highest waterfall is Yosemite Falls at 2,425 feet. It is the fifth-highest waterfall in the world.

- Yosemite's largest glacier is Lyell Glacier. Discovered by John Muir in 1871, it is also the second largest glacier in the Sierra Nevada.

- El Capitan is the park's highest rock face, measuring 3,000 feet high from the base.

- Yosemite has a great diversity of species: ninety different mammals, more than 262 kinds of birds, thirty-three amphibians and reptiles, six native fishes, 1,450 flowering plants, and thirty-seven tree species.

- Some of the species in Yosemite are protected, including forty animals and a total of 109 plant species have special plant status as either a species of concern or as rare.

- The giant sequoia tree, standing as tall as a thirty-story building, is the largest living thing in Yosemite—and the oldest.

Chapter Notes

Chapter One

1. Yosemite National Park, "Archaeology in Yosemite Valley," National Park Service.
2. Dan Anderson, "Yosemite Online Library—Yosemite Indians." Yosemite Conservancy.
3. Carl Parcher Russell, *One Hundred Years in Yosemite* (Yosemite National Park: Yosemite Association, 1992).
4. Dayton Duncan and Ken Burns, *The National Parks: America's Best Idea* (New York: Alfred A. Knopf, 2011).
5. Frederick Law Olmsted, *Yosemite and the Mariposa Grove: A Preliminary Report, 1865* (Yosemite National Park: Yosemite Association, 2009).
6. Dan Anderson, "Origin of the Word Yosemite," Yosemite Conservancy.

Chapter Two

1. Yosemite National Park, "Park Statistics," National Park Service.
2. Ibid.
3. Pacific Crest Trail Association, "Media Fact Sheet."
4. Yosemite National Park, "Mariposa Grove of Giant Sequoias," National Park Service.
5. Kari Cobb, Yosemite National Park Public Affairs Specialist (personal communication, October 30, 2013).
6. California State Parks, "Big Tree Life Cycle," State of California.
7. Yosemite National Park, "Mariposa Grove Winter Trails," National Park Service.
8. Douglas Brinkley, *The Wilderness Warrior: Theodore Roosevelt and the Crusade for America* (New York: Harper, 2009), ch. 19.

Chapter Three

1. Steven P. Medley, *The Complete Guidebook to Yosemite National Park* (Yosemite National Park: Yosemite Conservancy, 2012), p. 58.
2. Bill Guyton, *Glaciers of California* (Berkeley: University of California Press, 1998), p. 83.
3. John Muir, "Yosemite Glaciers (1871)." The Sierra Club.
4. Guyton, p. 131.
5. Ibid., pp. 85–86.
6. Alfred Runte, *Yosemite: The Embattled Wilderness* (Lincoln: University of Nebraska Press, 1990), p. 81.
7. Kurtis Alexander, "Rim Fire Cause: Hunter's Illegal Campfire," *San Francisco Chronicle,* September 5, 2013.
8. Incident Information System, "Rim Fire." National Wildlife Coordinating Group.

Chapter Four

1. Joseph Grinnell and Tracy Irwin Storer, "Sierra Mountain Beaver" in *Animal Life in the Yosemite* (Berkeley: University of California Press, 1924).
2. Duane Furman, "Summer Finds at Fairmead," Fossil Discovery Center of Madera County.
3. Yosemite National Park, "Bears." National Park Service.

Chapter Five

1. Yosemite National Park, "Park Statistics." National Park Service.

Works Consulted

Alexander, Kurtis. "Rim Fire Cause: Hunter's Illegal Campfire," *San Francisco Chronicle,* September 5, 2013. http://www.sfgate.com/science/article/Rim-Fire-cause-hunter-s-illegal-campfire-4789468.php

Anderson, Dan. "Origin of the Word Yosemite," July 10, 2011. Yosemite Conservancy. http://www.yosemite.ca.us/library/origin_of_word_yosemite.html

——. "Yosemite Online Library—Yosemite Indians," July 10, 2011. Yosemite Conservancy. http://www.yosemite.ca.us/library/ahwahneechee.html

"Beautiful but Deadly: Water in Yosemite," Yosemite National Park. http://www.youtube.com/watch?v=hzdIIxECONs&list=PL8F902DF131E49EBC

Bingaman, John W. "The Ahwahneechees: A Story of the Yosemite Indians (1966)," Yosemite Conservancy. http://www.yosemite.ca.us/library/the_ahwahneechees/chapter_1.html

Brinkley, Douglas. *The Wilderness Warrior: Theodore Roosevelt and the Crusade for America.* New York: Harper, 2009.

Brower, Kenneth. *Yosemite: An American Treasure.* Washington, D.C.: National Geographic Society, 1990.

"California Indian Acorn Culture—Background," National Archives.

California State Parks. "Big Tree Life Cycle," State of California.

"Dates of Statehood," NOAA Coastal Services Center.

Duncan, Dayton, and Ken Burns. *The National Parks: America's Best Idea.* New York: Alfred A. Knopf, 2011.

Furman, Duane. "Summer Finds at Fairmead, October 17, 2007," Fossil Discovery Center of Madera County.

Great Basin National Park. "Organic Act of 1916," National Park Service. http://www.nps.gov/grba/parkmgmt/organic-act-of-1916.htm

Grinnell, Joseph, and Tracy Irwin Storer. "Sierra Mountain Beaver" in *Animal Life in the Yosemite.* Berkeley: University of California Press, 1924.

Guyton, Bill. *Glaciers of California.* Berkeley: University of California Press, 1998.

Incident Information System. "Rim Fire," National Wildlife Coordinating Group.

Medley, Steven P. *The Complete Guidebook to Yosemite National Park.* Yosemite National Park: Yosemite Conservancy, 2012.

Muir, John. "Yosemite Glaciers," The Sierra Club.

——. *The Yosemite* (1912), Yosemite Conservancy. http://www.yosemite.ca.us/john_muir_writings/the_yosemite/

Olmsted, Frederick Law. *Yosemite and the Mariposa Grove: A Preliminary Report, 1865.* Yosemite National Park, CA: Yosemite Association, 2009.

Pacific Crest Trail Association. "Media Fact Sheet." http://www.pcta.org/media/media-fact-sheet/

Runte, Alfred. *Yosemite: The Embattled Wilderness.* Lincoln: University of Nebraska Press, 1990.

Russell, Carl Parcher. *One Hundred Years in Yosemite.* Yosemite National Park: Yosemite Association, 1992.

Yosemite National Park. National Park Service. https://www.nps.gov/yose/index.htm

Books

DeFries, Cheryl L. *What Are the 7 Natural Wonders of the United States?* Berkeley Heights, NJ: Enslow Publishers, Inc., 2013.

Dell, Pamela. *Welcome to Yosemite National Park.* Chanhassen, MN: The Child's World, 2007.

Lasky, Kathryn. *John Muir: America's First Environmentalist.* Candlewick Press, 2014.

Latham, Donna. *Mountains.* White River Junction, VT: Nomad Press, 2011.

McHugh, Erin. *National Parks: A Kid's Guide to America's Parks, Monuments, and Landmarks.* New York: Black Dog & Leventhal Publishers, 2012.

McKenzie, Precious. *Glaciers.* Vero Beach, FL: Rourke Publishing, 2011.

On the Internet

The National Parks—America's Best Idea
   http://www.pbs.org/nationalparks/

Parks and Nature—Yosemite Sequoias Need Fire

Yosemite National Park—For Kids
   http://www.nps.gov/yose/forkids/index.htm

backcountry (BAK-kun-tree)—An area so wild and rugged that roads cannot be built through it.

climate (KLIY-mit)—The average weather in a place over a period of years.

deciduous (dih-SID-joo-us)—A plant or shrub that loses its leaves and regrows them every year.

elevation (el-eh-VAY-shun)—Height of land above sea level.

endangered (en-DAYN-jerd)—So rare that the population or species could soon die off.

erode (ee-ROHD)—To break down over time, usually from wear by wind or water.

evergreen (EH-ver-green)—A tree or shrub that keeps its leaves all year.

glacier (GLAY-shur)—A large body of ice formed as layers of snow pack together over time; it moves slowly downhill under its own weight.

habitat (HAB-ih-tat)—The place where certain types of plants and animals normally live.

hibernate (HY-ber-nayt)—To enter a sleeplike state in which the body slows down to save energy during the winter.

magma (MAG-muh)—Liquid rock that erupts below Earth's surface.

Mariposa (mayr-ih-POH-sah)—Spanish for "butterfly," it is the name of the California county in which the giant sequoia trees grow.

scavenge (SKAA-venj)—To eat the meat of animals that are already dead; or, to eat trash.

sierra (see-AYR-uh)—A mountain range with jagged peaks.

American Dipper

PHOTO CREDITS: P.1—Randy Lemione; p. 4—King of Heartsv; pp. 6, 7, 8, 9, 10, 24, 25, 27 —nps.gov; p. 12—Dilliff, loc. gov; p. 15—blmcalifornia; p. 16—Vicente Villamon; p. 17—David Fulmer; p. 18—Don Graham; p. 19—Justin Vidamo; p. 20—terabass; p. 26—Mad Kramers; p. 28—LAcounty.gov, Rennett Stowe; p. 29—Jeff B; p. 30—J Wanamaker; p. 32—Arne List; p. 33—US Fish and Wildlife Services; p. 36—Mike Murphy; p. 37—Victor R. Ruiz; p. 38—Giorgio Galeotti; p. 40—Matt Deavonport. All other photos—Public Domain. Every measure has been taken to find all copyright holders of material used in this book. In the event any mistakes or omissions have happened within, attempts to correct them will be made in future editions of the book.